6-16

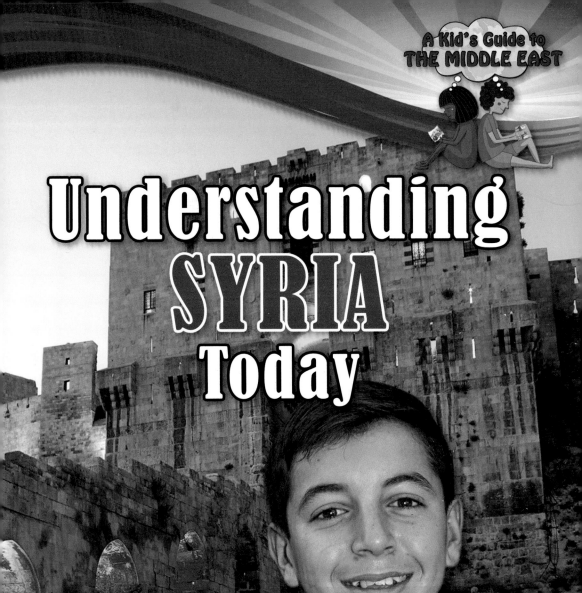

A Kid's Guide to
THE MIDDLE EAST

Understanding
SYRIA
Today

SYRIA

Michael Capek

Understanding Afghanistan Today
Understanding Iran Today
Understanding Iraq Today
Understanding Israel Today
Understanding Jordan Today
Understanding Lebanon Today
Understanding Palestine Today
Understanding Saudi Arabia Today
Understanding Syria Today
Understanding Turkey Today

Maydan

'Ayn al 'Arab

Amudah
Al Qamishli Suburzah Qhwadiyah
'Aradah al Kabnrah

Al Malikh

Jarabulus

Re's al Ayn

A'aze
'Afrine Tall Rifat
Jawban Bayk
Gerah Gawzak
Tall Abyad

Saluq

Al Hasakah

Curcurum
Al Bab
Monbij

'Ayn 'Isö

Gantari

Ash Shadadah

Halab (Aleppo)

Harim

As Sefirah

Dayr Hafir

Kassab

Idlib
Jisr ash Shughur
Ariha
Seraqib

Umm al 'Amud

Ar Raqqah
Madinat ath Thawrah (Tabqah)
Judaydat Khabur

Al Haffah

Jadid Ma'din

Al Ladhiqiyah (Latakia)
Al Qardahah

As Suwara

Al Tibni

Baniyas
Muhradah
Suran

Salamiyah

Syria

Dayr az Zawr

Busayrah

Masyaf
Hamah
Al Mashrafah
Jubb al Jarrah

Tartus

Al Mayadin
Al 'Asharah

Al Hamidiyah
Hims
Mukherram al Fawqani

As Sukhnah

Al Qusayr
Furqlus
Tiyas
Tadmus

Shincher

Hisyah

Abu Kama

Yabrud

Dayr 'Atiyah

Bi'r al 'Ulayyaniyah

Ma'lula

Rankus
Ar Ruhaybah

Ad Dimas
Dumayr

Sab' Abar

Qatana
Damascus

Buraq

Al Qunaytirah

Qasim

Shaykh Miskin

Ash Shajarah
As Suwayda

Der'a

Mafrak
Irbid

TURKEY

SYRIA

LEBANON — IRAQ

PALESTINE

IRAN

AFGHANISTAN

ISRAEL

JORDAN

SAUDI
ARABIA

Mitchell Lane
PUBLISHERS

Printing   1   2   3   4   5   6   7   8   9

Library of Congress Cataloging-in-Publication Data
Capek, Michael.
 Understanding Syria today / by Michael Capek.
      pages cm. — (A kid's guide to the Middle East)
 Includes bibliographical references and index.
 ISBN 978-1-61228-646-4 (library bound)
 1. Syria—Juvenile literature. I. Title.
 DS93.C37 2014
 956.91—dc23
                                                                              2014008839
eBook ISBN: 9781612286693

PUBLISHER'S NOTE: The fictionalized narrative used in portions of this book are an aid to comprehension. This narrative is based on the author's extensive research as to what actually occurs in a child's life in Syria. It is subject to interpretation and might not be indicative of every child's life in Syria. It is representative of some children and is based on research the author believes to be accurate. Documentation of such research is contained on pp. 60–61.

The Internet sites referenced herein were active as of the publication date. Due to the fleeting nature of some web sites, we cannot guarantee they will all be active when you are reading this book.

To reflect current usage, we have chosen to use the secular era designations BCE ("before the common era") and CE ("of the common era") instead of the traditional designations BC ("before Christ") and AD (*anno Domini*, "in the year of the Lord").

PBP

CONTENTS

BOLD words in text can be found in the glossary

Introduction

Marhaba! Ahlan wa sahlan! (mar-HA-buh ah-lahn-wah-SAH-lahn) Hello! Welcome!

Those are words you will hear often if you visit Syria. It's true! Syrians are famous for their hospitality, or treating visitors with kindness and respect. That might mean offering food, a comfortable place to rest, or help in times of need. It's always been part of the Arab culture to make guests feel welcome. In Syria it's more a way of life.

It began in ancient times. Syria's location in the Middle East made it a popular place. For centuries, people from all over the region stopped in Syria on their way to someplace else. That made Syria's early cities shopping centers for the world. All that buying and selling made Syria's merchants rich. And making all sorts of different people feel welcome made Syrian hospitality famous.

Now, all of this may come as a surprise to someone who has only learned about Syria from watching or reading the news in the past few years. The fact is, Syria is in the middle of a terrible war. Syria's people and its government are battling one another. No one seems to be acting in a very kind or respectful way right now.

Of course, all wars are hard to understand while they're happening. This one is even more confusing because outside forces have also joined the fighting. Some call these foreign groups "terrorists." Others call them "heroes." All sides believe their cause is the right one.

To most Syrians, who's right and who's wrong is less important now than just staying alive. Since it started in 2011,

Syria—Now and Then

the war has taken more than one hundred thousand lives.[1] Many of the dead were not soldiers on any particular side of the war. They were just ordinary men, women, and children who happened to be in the way when bombs fell and shooting started. By early 2014, more than two million **refugees** had escaped to neighboring countries.[2] Many millions more were homeless, trying to find shelter wherever they could. In a small nation that is only about the size of North Dakota, shelter is not easy to find.

For Syria, one could say, the past is the present. Because for Syria, war is nothing new. War followed by a short time of peace, repeated over and over—that is pretty much Syria's story. It's sad but true. Why this is so is as much about geography as anything else. Syria's position in the center of the Middle East has always made it an easy target. Syria's rich trading cities also attracted kings greedy for more wealth. But rulers and warriors fight for many reasons other than just money. Sometimes wars are about religion or power or freedom.

Although many people are fighting for many different reasons in the current war, we can be sure of one thing. Like all the others, this war will end someday. It may not make things any easier now, but it does provide some hope. Peace will come to Syria once again.

So, like Sabeen in chapter one, many of Syria's citizens believe it's best to face the harsh realities of "now," but still remember life as it was "then." That makes it possible to imagine how things certainly will be again one day.

Syrian refugees crowd into tents in Lebanon, near the border of Syria. As of April 2014, the United Nations estimates that more than one million people are living in Lebanon as refugees from the war.

CHAPTER 1
A Day with Sabeen

Back home in Aleppo, Syria, Sabeen was usually the first one out of bed in the morning. Here in Lebanon, she still is.

She used to get up early to study for exams, which she still hopes to take in two years. She was in seventh grade when the war in Syria started. She wants to go on to high school and then to college someday. To do that, she has to pass the tests after ninth grade.

For the past year and a half, Sabeen has been living in a makeshift camp in Lebanon. She came here in 2012 with her mother, brother, and baby sister. They came with thousands of others to escape the terror and bloodshed. Her father is still in Syria. He's not fighting in the war. He's trying to find his brothers and other family members in Damascus to help them get out, too.

There's a local school nearby where she could go, if the school had room for her. But Sabeen has decided she must do what she can for her family here. They need money badly. That's why she gets up before dawn to go to work. Both she and her younger brother Adad have worked on farms that hire children to pick fruit and vegetables. Shops and factories want child workers, too. Adad is eight and doesn't work every day, but Sabeen never misses a chance. School will just have to wait.

"Home" in this camp is a tent with a small stove in one corner. Beds are boards stretched atop cement blocks. Sabeen and Adad share the tent with their mother and baby sister,

A mother cares for her two young children in a Lebanese refugee camp. Although living conditions aren't fancy in these camps, most families are grateful to have a place to stay, far from the fighting in Syria.

Fatima. They are lucky to have a warm place where they can all spend the winter together. They have heard stories of other camps in Lebanon, Iraq, Turkey, and Jordan. Some are not as nice as this one. So many Syrians have escaped to neighboring countries looking for safety. It's hard for those nations to find clean, dry places to put everybody. And more refugees are arriving every day.

Sabeen's mother gets up and fixes her some cold bread and fruit for breakfast. Breakfast back at home was a hot spicy bread called *manakeesh* and a steaming cup of sweet tea. It was also a time for the family to gather before going to work and school. She misses that more than she misses the food.

Her mother works with other women around the camp for no pay. There aren't many men around. The women try to help each other by caring for the sick or watching each other's children. Many women are trying to find jobs, but local farmers and shops prefer to hire children. Kids will work for less money than adults, and they can be hired quickly.

Trucks arrive just after sunrise to take children to different places to work for the day. Sabeen climbs aboard with many others. Today, the ride isn't long. A rug factory not far from the camp needs as many girls as they can get. Girls' fingers are small and quick. For eight hours of work they might make 6,000 Lebanese pounds.[1] That's about $4 in the US. Sabeen is delighted. Sitting and weaving for hours is much easier than carrying heavy baskets filled with eggplants, pomegranates, or olives all day.

While her fingers fly, Sabeen's mind wanders. Thinking about the past helps pass the time.

Suddenly, Sabeen is back at her public school in Aleppo. She's wearing her green school uniform, standing with her classmates in the schoolyard. Girls and boys stand at opposite ends of the yard. All the classes join in singing Syria's national anthem, "Guardians of the Homeland." They all face the Syrian flag and a huge picture pasted on a wall in front of them. It's a picture of Syria's President, Bashar al-Assad, smiling and waving. "We must love and support our president, no matter what," the teacher says. Everyone turns and marches into the building. That's how every school day back home begins.[2]

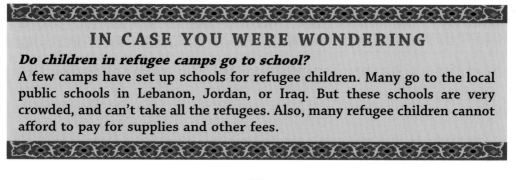

IN CASE YOU WERE WONDERING

Do children in refugee camps go to school?
A few camps have set up schools for refugee children. Many go to the local public schools in Lebanon, Jordan, or Iraq. But these schools are very crowded, and can't take all the refugees. Also, many refugee children cannot afford to pay for supplies and other fees.

Syrian children are happy for the chance to draw and play at a UN refugee center. Most refugees from the Syrian war are women and children.

Inside the dull, gray building, the teacher starts lessons. Sabeen shares her desk with three other girls. There are fifty students in her class. Science is Sabeen's favorite subject. Reading, writing, math, history, government, and Islamic religion are also taught.

The day at the Lebanese factory wears on. Sabeen works steadily, but her mind and heart keep drifting back to Syria. To pass the time, she tells herself stories. She relives good times and bad. She thinks about favorite places she visited, foods she ate, and people she knew. She wonders about the war and Syria's future. The stories and the memories get her through the long day.

FUN AND PLAY IN SYRIA

Kids in Syria like to play with many of the same things kids in other parts of the world do. Those who can afford computers play games on them. Soccer (kids in Syria call it "football") balls are seen everywhere in Syria, too. Many kids join school or league teams. But most just play for fun, in the streets and fields near their homes.[3] Of course, the war has interrupted many outdoor activities.

Girls in Syria love a doll called Fulla (foh-LAH). She has dark skin and eyes and comes with long dresses and a head covering. She looks more like most Syrian girls than dolls from Western countries do. Girls like American-style fashion dolls, too. But many parents prefer Fulla because she has "Muslim values."[4]

Fulla has many accessories such as umbrellas, bicycles, cameras, CD players, and swimming pools. She was modeled after Muslim women, and wears fashionable, modest clothing that is common in the Middle East.

Aleppo, Syria, is one of the oldest and most beautiful cities in the world. It has been the scene of a great deal of fighting during the recent war.

CHAPTER 2
Land of Sand and Water

When Sabeen thinks of home, she thinks of the desert. She lived in Aleppo, the largest city in Syria. But no matter where you live in Syria, you're never very far from the desert. Sabeen knew it well and loved it. Out in the hot, barren countryside, she found it easy to imagine what crossing the desert must have been like for people long ago.

The Camel Caravan

In one dream, Sabeen is with a **caravan** as it plods along. The camels snort and groan as they walk in single file across the burning sand. They're suffering in the early afternoon heat. They've been traveling since before sunrise with four-hundred-pound packs on each of their backs, and they're tired and cranky. The drivers are weary, too, but they walk beside the camels now instead of riding.

They're close to the end of their long journey. The drivers don't want to do anything now that might make the animals stop or lie down. If they did that the camels probably would not get up again. How would they ever get their goods to the **souks** of Damascus without camels, the men wonder? How would they carry the things they'll buy there back home again? These camels are everything to them, their very lives.

Men and animals walk on, peering into the distance. Suddenly someone calls out, "Green! I see green!" The men cup their hands around their eyes to shade them from the glare. "I see it, too!" someone else yells. "Palm trees," another calls excitedly. The camels lift their long necks and sniff the hot breeze. They begin to walk faster. The men must pull hard on their lead ropes to keep them from running. It has been many days since the camels have had anything to eat or drink. Their limp and sagging humps show it. They can hardly wait to get to the sweet fruit trees, shade, and cool flowing water they smell.

In the distance, a fuzzy line of green slowly emerges on the dull brown horizon. "Damascus!" the men shout happily. "Allah be praised! We have made it!"[1]

The Desert

At school, Sabeen learned much more about the arid Syro-Arabian Desert. For one thing, it makes up about two-thirds of modern Syria.[2] It also stretches into Saudi Arabia, Jordan, and Iraq, covering about two hundred thousand square miles (five hundred thousand square kilometers) in all.

Much of the desert is sand. But the area is also very rocky, and much of it is hard-packed, baked mud. Rain and even snow sometimes fall on the desert. But it still gets less than six inches (152 millimeters) of rainfall each year. Temperatures may soar to 115ºF (46ºC) or higher in the summer. And in the short winter, the desert can be very cold and windy, especially at night.

IN CASE YOU WERE WONDERING

Are souks still found in Syria today?

It's still possible to visit souks in the Old City section of Damascus. Aleppo, too, has a huge area where shops and stalls look, sound, and smell much the same as they did a thousand years ago. The alleys within the covered souks in Aleppo stretch for eight miles (thirteen kilometers). People come from all over the world to sample their endless delights. Sadly, much of the fighting of the current war has taken place in Damascus and Aleppo, and a fire destroyed parts of Aleppo's souks in 2012. But somehow business still goes on as it has for centuries.

In this Bedouin village, handmade houses called beehive houses protect their residents from the rapidly changing temperatures outside. Beehive houses are made of mud bricks, and are common in the arid northwestern parts of Syria, near Aleppo and Hama. Mud is practically the only building material available there.

This desert is the traditional home of the Bedouins (BED-oo-ins). These people are mostly **nomads**. They live in tents and move around a great deal. Bedouins are living examples of their ancestors' ancient lifestyle. Over time, many Bedouins settled in cities and towns, but some Bedouins still hang onto their wandering way of life. They herd camels, sheep, and goats, and sell meat, milk, and cheese. They sometimes wander into Damascus and other towns to buy and sell. But even today, they prefer to roam out in the desert areas much of the year, just as they have for thousands of years.

Water

Sabeen was surprised to learn that, in spite of its vast desert, Syria actually has a great deal of water. Rainfall mainly flows from the higher mountainous areas of the country. Mountains are important because they pull water from humid air as it passes over them. These form a narrow rim that arches from the country's southwestern end, up along its western side, and across its northwestern border with Turkey.

The Jabal an-Nusayriyah, or Coastal Mountain Range, stands like a western wall along the Mediterranean Sea. The Jabal al-Druze Mountains in Syria's southwest are eroded volcanoes that stopped erupting long ago. The Anti-Lebanon Mountains in the west are Syria's highest. Mount Hermon in this range rises to 9,232 feet (2,814 meters). To the south of Mount Hermon, along Syria's border with Israel, a high, rocky plateau forms the Golan Heights. Syria's lowest point is here, too, a body of water called Lake Tiberias or the Sea of Galilee.

The rainfall from the mountains runs down into the rivers. The Orontes enters southwestern Syria near Homs. Twenty-nine miles (forty-six kilometers) to the north of Homs, it drives the famous *noria* waterwheels in the city of Hama before continuing through northwestern Syria and into Turkey. The Barada River rises in the Anti-Lebanon Mountains and flows towards Damascus to the southeast. When the water reaches the low desert plain, it splits and fans out like thin, wiggling fingers. These streams create the rich al-Ghouta Oasis. An **oasis** is an island of fertile green in the desert, a place where water can be found in an otherwise dry region. That brilliant green space has greeted travelers for centuries as they emerged from the desert.[3]

Damascus is the capital of Syria, but Aleppo is its largest city. Close to three million people live in Aleppo. Both cities are built on oases. Is it any wonder that people have always thought of these cities as paradise on earth? Some people even believe Damascus now stands where the Garden of Eden once was.

IN CASE YOU WERE WONDERING

What were norias used for?
The norias are huge waterwheels, once used for irrigation at Hama. They're huge, up to sixty-six feet (twenty meters) high, and they can be heard for miles. The sound comes from the creaking of wet wood as the norias turn in the river current. The sound has sometimes been described as a humming, roaring, or snoring.

The Euphrates is Syria's longest and most important river. It flows south from Turkey, through Syria, and into Iraq. The river is about 1,728 miles (2,781 kilometers) long in all, though only about 420 miles (680 kilometers) of it is inside Syria. This slim band of water produces fertile land for wheat, cotton, and oil and is home to much of Syria's wildlife.[4]

Water from the Euphrates **irrigates** fields all along its course. Syria has built three dams on the Euphrates since 1973. These provide **hydroelectric** power, and also form lakes. The Tabqa, the largest of Syria's dams along the Euphrates, formed Lake al-Assad, which is about fifty miles (eighty kilometers) long. Al-Jabbul is a natural saltwater lake that is located just east of Aleppo. The lake is about twelve miles (twenty kilometers) long. Many of Syria's lakes provide drinking water for humans and animals. They also provide fun and relaxation activities, such as boating, swimming, and fishing.

In the middle of the desert, the land along the Euphrates River forms a ribbon of green. The river irrigates the nearby land, creating fertile soil for crops.

SYRIA'S PLANTS AND ANIMALS

The delicate balance between water and desert creates a unique home for plant and animal life. Elephants, lions, ostriches, wild donkeys, and the Arabian oryx (a kind of antelope) once roamed the deserts, plains, and mountainsides of Syria. Sadly, most of those animals became extinct before the twentieth century or are endangered today. Although the Syrian brown bear can still be found in other parts of the Middle East, this species recently became extinct in Syria.

Today, water birds—pelicans, ducks, geese, and flamingos—live along the Euphrates and other rivers. Eagles, falcons, and buzzards hunt in the valleys and along the edges of the great desert.

Desert animals include the gazelle and the jerboa, a small desert rodent with enormous ears that hops like a kangaroo. Snakes, lizards, and scorpions are common, too. Golden hamsters are native to northern Syria, where they threaten farmers' crops. Because of this, the farmers trap or poison them, and they may be endangered soon. Luckily, in 1930, a scientist dug up the den of a golden hamster in Syria. The majority of pet hamsters in the world today are the descendants of the babies he found.

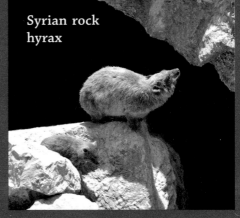

Syrian rock hyrax

Camels, goats, and sheep are raised throughout the country for meat and milk. Arabian horses have always been prized for their speed, beauty, and grace. Many are still bred by nomadic Bedouins or by breeders on farms in Syria.

Forests exist mainly in the mountains, and are largely made up of pine, oak, and cedar trees. Pistachio nuts and lemons grow in many parts of the country and are important ingredients in Syrian cooking. They are also exported to other countries. Forests once were dense, but many trees were cut down in earlier centuries. People needed wood for building and for fuel. Syria has a **reforestation** project in place now to replace the trees that were lost.

The desert ruins of Palmyra are said to be the most spectacular in Syria. This city was once the center of a vast empire. It was the home of Zenobia, a proud warrior queen who ruled all of Syria and Egypt during the third century. The ancient site is about 140 miles (225 kilometers) northeast of Damascus.

CHAPTER 3
The Past is the Present

It's 2011, a brilliant spring day in northwestern Syria. Sabeen and her classmates stare at the brown, sunbaked plain. They're on a field trip to the ruins of Ebla, thirty-five miles (fifty-six kilometers) southwest of Aleppo. "Imagine, if you can, a massive city of 250,000 people right here," their teacher says. "Great buildings and houses, now all gone. The king's palace had walls fifteen meters (fifty feet) high. Ebla was the center of a mighty kingdom hundreds of years before Abraham." The girls gasp with surprise. They have studied the early prophets of Islam and know that Abraham probably traveled through Syria sometime between 1700 and 2100 BCE.

Sabeen, working at her factory table two years later, smiles. She is still excited thinking of that day. Her home city of Aleppo, she learned, is even older. And Damascus, to the south, may be older than both of them. Everywhere in Syria, it seems, the past is always right under one's feet.

Ancient Times
From the fifteenth century BCE to the second century CE, many great empires rose and fell in Syria. These include the Egyptians, Hittites, Assyrians, Babylonians, Persians, Greeks, and Romans. Mighty as their soldiers and kings were, only a few traces of those empires remain in Syria today.

What motivated all these world powers to wage war on Syria? The answer is found in Syria's location. Wedged in, as it is, between nations of the Middle East, Syria has always been a land to cross. Its cities were prizes to be fought over.

Located at the far eastern end of the Mediterranean (med-i-tuh-REY-nee-uhn) Sea, Syria was in the perfect position for trade. Its cities, mainly Damascus and Aleppo, became trade centers for the rest of the world. Wealth poured into Syria.

The riches waiting in Syrian cities also attracted kings and emperors. They sent armies along trade routes to get it. War after war thundered and roared like storms sweeping out of the desert. When the wars ended, a new king or emperor ruled Syria. New people came to live in the cities, too, adding to the mix of customs and ideas that Syria has always been known for.

Islam and the Crusades

One of the most important ideas came to Syria from Palestine. Christianity, a new religion, arrived peacefully during the first century CE. It joined a number of other religions that people practiced in Greater Syria, which was much larger than the modern-day country.

A new kind of conqueror arrived during the seventh century CE. These warriors did not come seeking riches. They fought to bring yet another religion called Islam to Syria. This new Arab religion, which was founded by the Prophet Muhammad (moo-HAM-uhd), changed everything.

The followers of this religion called themselves Muslims, which means "one who submits to God's will." Warriors fought

IN CASE YOU WERE WONDERING

Why is Ebla so important?

Scientists exploring Ebla have found a library with thousands of tablets with written records on them. Writers called scribes made these by pressing sharp sticks or pieces of bone into wet clay. The tablets revealed what everyday life was like for people in the city, and gave historians new information about the Middle East as it existed over four thousand years ago.

with great emotion because they believed they were fighting God's war. After this, Islam became the main religion of Syria.

By the eighth century CE, the Islamic empire included parts of modern-day Spain, northern Africa, the Middle East, and India. It was more than twice as large as the Roman Empire had ever been.

The Umayyads (oo-MAHY-ads), leaders of the second **caliphate**, or Islamic state, made Damascus their capital. The majestic Umayyad **Mosque** they built there was one of the first great worship centers of Islam. Damascus also became one of the two main starting points of the yearly *Hajj*. This trip to Mecca was (and still is) an important part of the Muslim religion.

Beginning around 1095, Christians battled Muslims for control of cities in Turkey, Palestine, and Syria. These wars, known as the Crusades, lasted for about two hundred years. Some of the most important of these battles were between Syrian Sultan Saladin and the English King Richard the Lionheart. Over the course of many battles, Saladin and Richard came to respect and admire one another. In 1192, the two leaders signed a truce. They agreed that Muslims would keep control of Jerusalem and Christian pilgrims would be allowed to visit their holy city any time they wished.

The Ottoman Empire

In 1516, the Ottomans won control of Syria. They were Muslim Turks from nearby Central Asia. But they did not come because Syria had once been a great Islamic center. To the Ottomans, Syria was just more land and people to rule. During the sixteenth century, under the rule of Suleiman (SOO-ley-mahn) the Magnificent, the Ottoman Empire became one of the most powerful states in the world. The massive Ottoman Empire included parts of Asia, the Middle East, southeastern Europe,

IN CASE YOU WERE WONDERING

Why did Saladin show kindness to Richard the Lionheart, an invader and bitter enemy?
Saladin believed that showing kindness to his opponents was a sign of strength, not weakness. Once when Richard was ill, Saladin sent his own doctor to take care of him. On another occasion, during battle, Richard's horse was killed. Saladin sent him two horses of his own.[1]

and North Africa. Constantinople (today's Istanbul, Turkey) was its capital city. Under their stern rule, Syria remained an Ottoman state for four hundred years.

By the twentieth century, though, many Arabs across the Middle East were tired of Ottoman rule. After World War I began, the Ottomans joined Germany and the Central Powers. On the other side, the Allies (the British, French, Russians, Americans, and others) asked a group of Syrian Arabs to fight the Ottomans. The Allies promised that if Germany and Ottoman Turkey were defeated in the war, the Arabs would get their independence. The Arab army won many battles against their Ottoman rulers and helped the Allies win the war.

But Arab joy quickly turned to anger. When the peace treaty ending World War I was signed, the Allies did not keep their promise. Instead, they divided up the old Ottoman Empire into many new nations. Syria was given to France as its colony. Its new borders made it a much smaller country. Syrian Arabs fought their new rulers, but the French were more powerful. Once again, Syrians were ruled by a foreign power. It was a bitter defeat after being so close to freedom.

World War II in the 1940s turned Syria into a battleground once again. When this war ended, France finally agreed to give up control of Syria, and in 1946, Syrians happily celebrated their first year of true independence. It appeared Syria's long history of war and foreign control was over.

THE UMAYYAD MOSQUE AND THE CRAC DES CHEVALIERS

Two sites that link Syria's past and present are the Umayyad Mosque in Damascus and the Crac des Chevaliers near Homs.

To make the Islamic capital even more special, Caliph Khaled ibn al-Walid built a magnificent place of prayer in Damascus in the beginning of the eighth century. He called it "a mosque the equal of which was never designed by anyone before me or anyone after me."[2] The Umayyad Mosque was built of stone and marble and decorated with gold. Outer and inner walls were covered with mosaics (moh-ZEY-iks). These are pictures made up of thousands of small pieces of glass, marble, and other shiny objects.

The Umayyad Mosque, also called the Great Mosque of Damascus, was one of the first great Islamic places of worship. The mosque was large enough for thousands of Muslims to gather and pray in at the same time. This mosque still stands today as a reminder of a time when Syria was the center of the Islamic world.

Another of Syria's great buildings is the Crac de Chevaliers, or "Castle of the Kurds." Most of the current structure was built during the twelfth century by Christian invaders during the Crusades. These were attacks by European warriors whose quest was to take back the holy cities of Greater Syria from Muslim control. All over the region, the invaders battled Muslim warriors. Wherever they could, they built strong castles. The Crac des Chevaliers was the largest and most important of these forts. The knights held the site until it became clear the Crusades were over in 1271. Today visitors can tour the site, which has been called "the finest castle in the world."[3]

Umayyad Mosque

Syria's President Bashar al-Assad speaks during a meeting of the Baath Party in Damascus. Since the war began, many world leaders have called for Assad to give up power in Syria.

CHAPTER 4
A Government at War

Like most kids in Syria, Sabeen knows many facts about her country's government. She knows, for instance, that the people of the Syrian Arab Republic are represented in the government by the *Majlis al-Shaab* (MAHJ-lis al-SHAHB) or People's Council. The council is made up of 250 members, elected for four-year terms. They suggest new laws, nominate presidential candidates, and approve the national budget. The current president is Bashar al-Assad, who was the only candidate in the 2007 election. The president must be a Muslim, and elections are held every seven years. The president appoints a vice president, a prime minister, a cabinet, and minor officials of the government.

Sabeen also understands that the president has many powers, including the power to declare war or a state of emergency. Syria has been a military government under "emergency law" since 1963. When Hafez al-Assad (father of Bashar al-Assad) became president in 1971, he maintained this state of emergency. This gave the president the power to do whatever he thought was necessary to protect the nation.[1] Bashar al-Assad ended those old laws in 2011, but created others. These still gave the president total power in Syria.[2]

Sabeen learned these things in lessons at school. But she still finds it hard to understand the present war. Why does the Syrian government appear to be fighting against its own people? How did such a war get started?

Arab Spring and the Boys of Daraa

One cold February afternoon in 2011, some boys between ten and fifteen years old were walking home along a street in Daraa in southwestern Syria. They were bored and decided to write graffiti on a wall. The words said something like, "Down with the government."

Later they explained that they had seen the words on TV. News reports about demonstrations in Egypt, Tunisia, and other Middle Eastern countries showed pictures of people shouting and carrying signs. People were calling these protests the "Arab Spring" movement.

The boys who wrote on the wall didn't really know much about the Arab Spring. They didn't understand that in Syria, no one may say or write anything against the Syrian government. President Assad's *mukhabarat* (mook-HOH-bay-ROHT), or secret police, have the power to arrest anyone who does—even children.[3]

On March 6, the boys were arrested and taken away. Police wouldn't tell the boys' parents where they had been taken. The families begged for help, but no one in power would listen. After nearly two weeks, people began to gather in the streets of Daraa. They demanded that government officials release the boys. Security forces met them and shot into the crowd. Three people were killed.[4]

The next day, thousands of people protested against the government at the funerals of those killed. More people died. Day after day, people marched and police fired at them. Finally, after two weeks in jail, the boys were released. They had been beaten and tortured. People all over Syria were outraged and took to the streets to protest. By October 2011, more than three thousand Syrians had died. Hundreds more were in jail just for speaking out against the attacks.[5]

These terrible incidents provided the opportunity many Syrians had been waiting for. They saw this as their chance to join other Arab nations in their fight for more freedom. Some members of Syria's military left their positions. They joined with the citizens and formed their own army. They vowed to overthrow Assad and stop government troops from killing more people. A group called the Syrian National Council organized, too. They were made up mostly of Muslims who had never liked President Assad or his Baath Party. Another group known as the Muslim Brotherhood joined them. Many other people formed small armies of their own, hoping to protect their homes and loved ones. Open warfare erupted in the streets of many cities. Soon, it became hard to tell who was fighting for or against the government.

By the beginning of 2014, around 130,000 Syrians had died in the fighting.[6] More than two million had left Syria, seeking safety in neighboring nations. Many of those refugees (like Sabeen) remained in camps in Jordan, Turkey, Iraq, and Lebanon. Others were staying in cities in those nations, where they rented homes or lived with local families.[7]

As 2014 dawned, the hope of Arab Spring 2011 had mostly faded. At the beginning, Syrian rebels only wanted freedom from their own government. But thousands of fighters from all over the region arrived in Syria to fight for one side or another.

IN CASE YOU WERE WONDERING

Is there any sign that the war in Syria might be ending soon?
In January 2014, the United Nations brought together people from all sides of Syria's war in Geneva, Switzerland. It was hoped that talking about their problems might make things better. It's still uncertain whether the meetings made any difference.[8]

A man holds a picture of Hafez al-Assad during a demonstration in support of the present government.

During January, various rebel groups appeared to attack helpless citizens and each other as much as they fought against the government.[9]

But one ray of hope still shone in the darkness. All sides agreed in early 2014 to meet for peace talks. As one former Syrian official said, "Everybody is tired, everybody realizes that he is not able to win over and wipe out the other party. Nobody is winning. There's a need on both sides to catch their breath."[10]

BASHAR AL-ASSAD

Growing up, Bashar al-Assad had no real interest in politics or the military. He was a quiet boy. Compared to his older brother, Bassel, Bashar seemed almost shy. Bassel was his father's favorite. He loved sports and action and trained to become a soldier, like his father. The boys' father, Hafez al-Assad, was Syria's president, and so would Bassel be one day. What lessons did the boys learn from watching their father?

In the 1970s, a group of Syrians called the Muslim Brotherhood began fighting against the government. In February 1982, they took control of Hama. Hafez ordered his army to attack the entire city. After nearly a month of artillery fire and bombings, the town was destroyed and more than ten thousand people were

Hama after the government attacked the city, 1982.

killed. Most of them, including many women and children, were not involved in the fight against the government or Hafez al-Assad. At this time, Bashar was in his final year of high school.

After studying engineering in college, Bassel went into the army. Bashar went to the University of Damascus to study medicine. He earned his degree in **ophthalmology** and continued his training at the Western Eye Hospital in London, England.

In 1994, Bassel died in a car accident. Immediately, Bashar went back home and started military training. Within five years he became a colonel in the Syrian Army. He also served as an assistant to his father.

When his father died in 2000, Bashar was elected president. He won easily, because no one else could run against him. Still, people hoped that the son would be less cruel than his father had been. Sadly though, recent history shows that Bashar al-Assad seems to have learned his father's lessons well.

Men praying in
the Umayyad
Mosque in
Damascus, Syria

CHAPTER 5
Religion

It's late morning at the factory. About this time back home, Sabeen would be in school, getting ready to go to her Islamic studies class. At her school, Christian students may also go to another room for lessons in their own religion.[1]

For Sabeen and her family, Islam is more than just a way to worship. It's a way of life that affects everything they do and say. They follow rules and customs that go back hundreds of years.

Muhammad and the Five Pillars of Islam

Islam began with the Prophet Muhammad. Muhammad was a successful merchant born about 570 CE in Mecca (in what is now Saudi Arabia). During the month of Ramadan, he went to pray in a cave on a mountain near Mecca. The angel Gabriel came to him with important messages from Allah (God). Muhammad wrote down the messages in the Koran (also spelled Quran). Those who believed the words of this book understood that Muhammad was Allah's prophet and holy messenger on earth. The religion Muhammad taught was called Islam; its followers called themselves Muslims.

The teachings of Islam include five basic things all Muslims must do. These are known as the Five Pillars of Islam.

First, Muslims must declare, "There is no god but Allah, and Muhammad is his prophet." They must also pray five times each day—before sunrise, after midday, in the middle of the afternoon, after sunset, and at bedtime. Third, believers must give to the poor and needy. Next, they must fast during

Ramadan. During this month, adult Muslims do not eat or drink between sunrise and sunset every day. Finally, they must make a journey, or Hajj, to Mecca at least once in their lifetime if they are able to.

Most Muslims follow these rules to the letter, as sacred duties. Other responsibilities are described in the Koran. These include being honest, humble, and modest in one's dress and actions. Modesty is very important for both genders, but particularly for girls and women. That is why many Muslim women wear long robes and veils that cover their legs, arms, and heads. Muslim girls must dress modestly, too. They usually don't start wearing head coverings until about ten or twelve.

An elderly Muslim man sits inside the Umayyad Mosque reading the Koran.

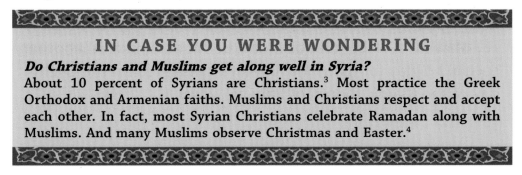

Many Muslim women and girls wear clothing that covers their heads and much of their bodies. But customs of dress are not as conservative in Syria as they are in some other Islamic nations.

In Syria, the rules of Islam are not followed as closely as in many other Islamic countries. People are free to practice their religion in many different ways. Many females wear clothes much like those Americans wear. Some cover their heads with scarves when they are in public and others do not.[2] This is not true in some other Islamic nations, where a person may be arrested for not praying, acting, or dressing properly.

Divisions of Islam

Muslims can be divided into two main divisions or sects—Sunni (SOON-ee) and Shia (SHEE-uh). The split between these two began after the death of Muhammad. Sunnis believed that the

IN CASE YOU WERE WONDERING

Do Christians and Muslims get along well in Syria?
About 10 percent of Syrians are Christians.[3] Most practice the Greek Orthodox and Armenian faiths. Muslims and Christians respect and accept each other. In fact, most Syrian Christians celebrate Ramadan along with Muslims. And many Muslims observe Christmas and Easter.[4]

next Islamic leader should be elected from among important Muslims. Shiites believed only direct relatives of Muhammad himself should lead the religion.

Today, Sunnis and Shiites worship in slightly different ways. Sunnis believe that it is possible for each person to understand Allah's teachings without the help of anyone else. Shiites believe that without an *imam* (ih-MAHM), or spiritual leader, it is impossible for them to fully understand or connect with Allah. Most Muslims in the world are Sunnis. The same is true in Syria, where 74 percent are Sunni and 13 percent are Shiites.[5]

The two forms of Islam have several different smaller branches, or types, also. Other sects are independent—neither Sunni nor Shiite. Some of the smaller Muslim branches and sects in Syria are Alawis (AL-uh-weez), Sufis (SOO-feez), and Druze (drooz).

Islamic Holidays

The feast celebration called Eid al-Fitr (ID-al-FIT-er) marks the end of Ramadan. It is one of the happiest times of the Islamic year. People visit relatives and friends for feasting and fun. Children get candy and gifts. For three days, Muslims celebrate in this way, enjoying all sorts of fancy foods and drinks.[6]

Even more important is Eid al-Adha (ID-al-AD-ha), the feast of sacrifice. This holiday comes at the end of the annual pilgrimage to Mecca. It is a day which commemorates Abraham's willingness to obey God's command. It's celebrated with feasting, parties, and many fun activities, especially for children.

Mawlid al-Nabi, the birthday of Muhammad, is another special holiday for many Muslims. It's celebrated on the twelfth day of the Islamic month of Rabi al-Awwal.

THE JOURNEY TO MECCA

Muslim pilgrims have been traveling to and from Mecca since the Arab conquest in the seventh century. There were many routes for the hard and dangerous journey. But perhaps the most popular route began in Damascus.

Thousands of pilgrims would gather in Damascus in the weeks before the trip was to begin. Bands of robbers would also gather all along the route. Hajjis were in danger from wild animals, floods, snow, sandstorms, and blazing heat. It was easy to get lost in the desert, too.[7] Each year, many travelers left Damascus and were never seen or heard from again.[8]

In the fifteenth century, Ottoman Sultan Suleiman the Magnificent made changes to make the long trip safer for pilgrims. At that time, forts were opened for pilgrims, which provided them with places to sleep, eat, worship, and receive medical treatment during their journey. Groups were organized and soldiers traveled along with them for protection.[9] Many merchants offered travel services, too. For a high price, they offered guides, guards, food, and even transportation. Other peddlers followed caravans to and from Mecca. When the travelers stopped, the sellers appeared, selling them water, food, and anything else they might need or want.[10]

From Damascus, a Hajji needed about thirty-five days to reach Mecca on foot (or on camelback). After a week in Mecca to perform the necessary ceremonies, pilgrims left for the thirty-five-day journey back. In all, it took more than two months to complete the Hajj.[11]

Muslim pilgrims at Mecca

Cars, trains, and air travel became the main method of pilgrimage in the twentieth century. But today, some Muslims still make their Hajjs the old-fashioned way—overland and on foot.[12]

Some Syrians still herd sheep and goats as their ancestors have always done.

CHAPTER 6
People and Crafts

As she works through the long afternoon, Sabeen's mind roams across borders and time. She remembers once seeing a dim, yellowed picture hanging in her Grandmother Tira's house. "Jaddati, who is that man?" Grandmother Tira looked lovingly at the photo for a long time. "That is my Grandfather Faroush. He was Kurdish." Then she said, very seriously, "He always used to tell me, 'Be swift if you are a hammer. Be patient if you are an anvil.'" Before Sabeen could ask, Grandmother added, "When you learn about the Kurds, you will understand the saying. Syria is a rich stew of peoples. All of them are special, but not all are made to feel that way."

The Arab Majority
Today, Arabic is the language most people speak in Syria. One exception is Aramaic. This was the language spoken in the region in ancient times, which is closely related to modern Arabic. It's still spoken in a few communities and villages in Syria. Some Syrians also speak Kurdish, Armenian, Turkish, French, and English.

Syria is a mixture of different peoples. Most Syrians (about 90 percent) are Arabs.[1] This term refers to people whose ancestors lived on the Arabian Peninsula (south of Syria) and spoke the Arabic language. Most Arabs are Muslims, as well.

Syrian Arabs take great pride in the history and culture of their people. Many wish they could join with other Arabs and work together for common goals. But such efforts have not gone well in the past. Syria's attempt to unite with Egypt to form the United Arab Republic in 1958, for instance, didn't work. The two nations became separate again in 1961. Although many Arabs have much in common, Arabs are also citizens of many different countries, with many different goals.

Minority Groups

Certain smaller groups who are not Arabs also live in Syria. These include Circassians, Assyrians, Armenians, Druze, and Kurds.

About one hundred thousand Circassians live in Syria. These people are Sunni Muslims who came to Syria from the Caucasus region of Russia in the mid-1800s. They consider themselves "outcasts" because they were forced to leave their Russian homelands to live in Ottoman territory. The Circassians hold onto many of their own customs such as folk dances and clothing styles.

About one million Assyrians live in Syria today. These are mostly Christians who speak Aramaic. This ancient language was spoken throughout the region before Arabic. It was the native language of Jesus Christ. The Assyrians came from Iraq in 1933 and settled along the Khabur River in northeastern Syria. The Assyrian settlement there consists of about thirty-five villages. The area is semi-desert, but the people have learned to irrigate fields. They are farmers who grow mostly cotton and wheat, and raise sheep and goats.

The Druze make up about 3 percent of the Syrian population. These people live mostly in the Jabal al-Druze. This is a rugged and mountainous region in southwestern Syria. Like Muslims, they honor Abraham, Jesus, and Muhammad, the three most important prophets of Islam. But the Druze believe in a deeper understanding of the meaning of the Koran, beyond the literal meaning. Most aspects of their worship are kept strictly secret.

Even some longtime members of the community are not included in its secrets.[2]

The largest group of non-Arabs are the Kurds. They have no home nation, but live in an area of the Middle East they call "Kurdistan." This region spans the borders of Turkey, Iraq, Iran, and Syria. In Syria, most Kurds live in the northeast corner of the country. Although Kurds are Sunni Muslims, they are not treated as equals in most of the places they live. In some places, including Syria, Kurds are not even allowed to build their own schools or publish books in their language. Various groups of Kurds have also had many conflicts with the governments of the countries they live in. In 2013 and 2014, one Kurdish political party, the Democratic Union Party (PYD), took advantage of the civil war by seizing control of the local governments in the Kurdish regions. The Syrian government's forces were too busy fighting in other parts of the country to respond.[3]

Syrian Crafts

The shops and souks of ancient Syria have always been home to some of the finest craftsmen in the world. Coppersmiths once pounded metal into practically any shape a customer wanted. Rugs, stained glass, pottery, leather, jewelry, perfumes, and fabrics could be found at any time in the shops of Damascus and Aleppo. Many craftsmen still work there using the same methods today.

Aleppo soap

Syrians are known worldwide for the soaps they have been making for hundreds of years. Aleppo craftsmen made the highest quality soap in the world using pure, natural olive

A souk in
Aleppo, Syria

oil. Europeans discovered Syrian soap in the eleventh century, when warriors brought it back from the Crusades. After that merchants traveled great distances to get it for their customers all over the world.[4]

The weaving of Damask fabric is another Syrian craft. Damask is a rich, colorful cloth made of silk, wool, or cotton. It's called Damask because around the twelfth century, traders from Europe first found the fabric in Damascus. It quickly became popular in European cities. Some of the cloth was made in Syria. But much of it probably came from further east in China, India, and Persia. These countries were known for producing fine silk fabric. They were also important stops along the web of trade routes called "The Silk Road." Damascus was at the western end of those roads and received goods from places thousands of miles away. Most traders from the West didn't speak Arabic, so they just assumed all things they bought in Syrian markets came from there.[5]

Crusaders facing Saladin's warriors in battle thought Arab swords were magical. Muslim blades almost never broke in battle the way the Christians' swords and knives did. The fact is, metal workers from Damascus had discovered a way of making steel so tough it was almost impossible to break. The secret technique involved adding carbon to the melted metal. Weapons makers in other countries soon learned the secret, but the metal is still called Damascus steel.

Art of the Written and Spoken Word

For centuries, Muslim artists have not been allowed to paint or draw pictures of people or animals. Muslims believe that doing this could encourage people to worship the beings in the pictures. Because of this, artists found other ways to create.

Calligraphy, or the art of handwriting, flourished during the Umayyad era (661–750) in Damascus. Scribes from all over the Islamic world gathered there to learn the art of writing verses from the Koran in beautiful Arabic script. Sometimes written in gold, these were often used as decorations in mosques, palaces, and private homes.[6]

Poetry has always been popular in Syria, too. Arabic is a musical language, and poems in Arabic have been written and read since ancient times. The Koran is a book of poetry. Verses from it have often been sung and recited aloud in public for years. The old Ottoman caliphs liked to keep poets in their courts, as well, to entertain and inspire. Poets could also write stirring poems about victories in battle or praise for a ruler's goodness and wisdom.[7]

Storytelling is another beloved Syrian tradition. For centuries storytellers called *hakawatis* (hak-uh-WAH-teez) were important members of every community. Long before television or movies, they were skilled actors who could make stories and

45

characters come alive. In modern times, a few hakawatis can still be found in coffeehouses and restaurants in Damascus and Aleppo. While customers drink beverages or eat meals, hakawatis recite exciting tales. Some may come from *A Thousand and One Nights*, like the famous story of "Aladdin's Wonderful Lamp." Others may be stories the hakawatis make up themselves. Listeners, young and old, don't care. They love them all.

IN CASE YOU WERE WONDERING

What folk dances do Syrians do?
Syrians dance the *dabkeh* (DEB-kuh) at every opportunity. It's a wild, stomping line dance, done to the beat of fast, loud music. It starts out slow, with everybody stepping and holding hands, moving in time together. The line moves forward or back, or from side to side, following a leader. There's always a great deal of laughing and shouting as the music and dancing gets faster and faster.[8]

CLOTHING IN SYRIA

In Syria, people wear many different types of clothing. Like Muslims in other nations, most Syrian people wear clothes that cover much of their bodies. Some men still wear Arab-style robes called kaftans and head coverings known as *kafiyeh* (keh-FEE-yeh). These were first worn by men in desert countries for protection from sun and blowing dust and sand. Today, many men still wear them, even those who don't work outdoors.[9] Many Syrian women and girls wear long dresses that cover their shoulders, arms, and legs. They also wear head coverings, called *hijabs* (hi-JAHBZ). Muslim women do this in keeping with Islamic customs of modesty. The traditional dress for women in Syria is called a *thob*. It is long and has triangular sleeves.

In many villages people wear special costumes for weddings and other celebrations. Bright colors and patterns are worn by certain tribes or ethnic groups. These fancy clothes help people feel connected to their past. Wearing them is a way of showing pride in old ways and customs.

Many Syrians, especially young people, wear modern Western clothes. These include shirts, dress pants, dresses, and skirts, much like Americans wear to school or work. Blue jeans and t-shirts are also seen in universities and big cities. But few people of any age wear anything that leaves their legs, shoulders, or upper arms bare. There are no laws against this type of clothing. It's just considered good taste to dress modestly.

A street vendor dressed in a t-shirt and jeans sells traditional Syrian clothing.

This array of bread and mezze dishes is a typical lunch in Damascus. Coffee or tea is part of most meals in Syria, too. So is the traditional waterpipe.

CHAPTER 7
Food and Holidays

Sabeen's work day is almost done. She's tired and hungry. In her daydreams, she sees herself waiting for Adad by the front gate after school. It's twelve thirty. School is over for the day. Adad always wants to stay and play football (Americans call it soccer) with other boys. He doesn't like a girl telling him what to do. Still, it's Sabeen's job as big sister to get him home. Adad doesn't complain much. Neither of them wants to be late for lunch.

Father comes home from his work at two thirty in the afternoon. Everyone is there waiting when he arrives. Surprise! Today he has brought Grandmother Tira with him from all the way across town. It feels like a holiday with her there. She's brought her amazing baba ghanoush (bah-bah-guh-NOOSH), a delicious eggplant dip. As always, the table is crowded with a dozen bowls and dishes filled with many different foods. Everyone grabs flatbread, rips it apart, and digs in, laughing and talking at the same time.

In Syria, family is everything. Every meal with your family is a celebration.

Sabeen longs for the day when they'll all be together around the table once again.

Mezze and Kibbeh

Almost every Syrian meal includes bread and small dishes, or *mezze* (MEH-zay). That's an Arabic word that means "taste," or "snack." Meals usually begin with breaking bread. Syrian bread is very thin and is not cut, but pulled apart by hand. The pieces of bread are used to dip and scoop up food.[1]

Mezze dishes include a wide variety of things to scoop up and dip into. They are served on many small plates scattered around the table. One dish might contain olives. Another might have baba ghanoush. There might also be tabouleh (tuh-BOO-luh), a finely chopped salad. Nearly every meal includes hummus, a dip made from chickpeas, and tahini (tuh-HEE-nee). Tahini is a sauce made of sesame seeds. This nutty-tasting paste is used by Syrians in dips, salads, and other sauces, or on its own.

Sometimes, mezze is the whole meal. Many times it's only the beginning—an appetizer, or pre-meal snack. That's why mezze plates and dishes are usually small.

A main course or entrée is likely to be lamb. It appears on Syrian tables more than any other meat. *Kibbeh* (KIB-beh) is one of the most common ways lamb is prepared. This is a mixture of ground lamb meat, onions, and cracked wheat. The mixture is shaped into oblong balls and fried. It's so popular, kibbeh is often called "the national dish of Syria."

Syrians love spices of all kinds and put them into everything they can. They add lots of garlic, cumin, and mint to their dishes. *Za'atar* (ZAH-ah-tahr) is a mixture of several different spices, mainly thyme mixed with oregano, sesame seeds, or dried sumac. This last ingredient is a lemony-sour berry that

IN CASE YOU WERE WONDERING

What do Syrian kids like to drink with snacks?
One popular drink in Syria is called *laban ayran*. This is made from plain yogurt, salt, and water. Sometimes other ingredients can be mixed in, such as mint, garlic, and sugar. Street sellers and fast food restaurants in many cities sell laban ayran. Whipped into a foam and poured over ice, laban ayran is a delicious, cooling sip on a hot day.

grows all over the Middle East. Za'atar is used in many ways. One of the most popular is as a topping for bread called manakeesh. It's something like pan pizza dough with a thick coating of za'atar. Syrian kids love manakeesh for breakfast, and they often carry leftovers to school for mid-morning snacks. It's also served in school cafeterias.[2]

Holiday Foods

Eating during Ramadan is special. The first things eaten after sunset by many Muslims are dates. That's believed to be the way Muhammad broke his Ramadan fast. Soup often follows. Later in the evening, most Muslims enjoy their main meal with family and friends.[3]

During Eid al-Fitr, at the end of the Ramadan fast, Muslims love to eat rich desserts and sweets. *Halva*, a rich candy made of tahini and honey, is one of these. *Kanafeh bel-jouz* is another Syrian holiday treat, made from a sweet cheese pastry and walnuts.[4]

Syrian Christians, too, celebrate their holidays with special foods. Catholic, Protestant, Armenian, and Greek Orthodox Christians in Syria observe Lent and Easter in somewhat different ways. Many fast, but not all day, as Muslims do. They don't eat milk or meat during Lent, the period before Easter. Instead they eat a variety of vegetarian dishes. On Easter they break their fasting with feasts that include roast lamb and all sorts of sweet treats. *Ma'amoul* are date pastries that are traditionally eaten at both Easter and Christmas.

Weddings and Special Occasions

One particularly special event for all Syrians is a wedding in the family. This is a time of great joy and excitement for children and adults. Like most happy times, weddings are celebrated with food—particularly sweets. At some traditional wedding parties, guests are given pastries and sugar-coated almonds. These represent everyone's wish of a sweet life for the bride and groom. People used to give goats or lambs as wedding gifts. That way the happy couple would always have plenty of milk and meat. Today, lamb is the main dish served at most wedding dinners.

It's a custom in some villages to serve *meghli*, a sweet cinnamon rice pudding, when a baby is born. When the baby gets its first tooth, the family eats sugar-coated almonds and chickpeas.[5]

Even a death in the family is observed with food and family in many places. Only water or unsweetened coffee is served with the feast given in honor of the deceased loved one. Most Syrians believe the soul stays around for forty days after death. It then begins its journey into the afterlife. At this time, another dinner is held in the person's memory.[6]

SYRIA'S DEAD CITIES

Scattered across Syria's barren north are the remains of hundreds of abandoned towns and cities. These "dead cities," or ghost towns, were once beautiful, active centers along Syria's busy northern trade routes. Thousands of people lived and worked in them. Now they're abandoned. Only ruined stone walls and broken columns remain. Sometime around 600–700 CE, the people who lived in them simply left. But why?

Experts now believe that around the sixth and seventh centuries Syria's trade routes changed suddenly. This would be the same as factories and stores in a city today suddenly closing their doors. People had to go elsewhere to find work and buy the things they needed.

Fortunately, the buildings they left behind are like time capsules. Scientists and historians study them to learn how people lived in ancient times. They are constantly finding new things in and under these old ruins. One of the most eerie and beautiful of these cities is Serjilla. The town has been deserted for about 1,500 years, but many of its stone buildings are incredibly well preserved. It's easy to imagine what the city would have been like long ago.

Today, with war raging in Syria, many of these old relics are in danger. Other important historical cities in Syria have already been damaged by the fighting. So far, most of the dead cities remain unhurt. They are far from big cities where most of the fighting has taken place. But also because of their remote location, the dead cities have come under another kind of attack. Refugees have been running to these ancient ruins, seeking shelter from the war.[7] Most people don't mean to harm these priceless, old places. Still, they can cause damage just by digging under things or moving ancient stones. Others, desperate for money, take the historic artifacts they find and sell them.

Serjilla, a "dead city" near Hama, Syria.

SESAME HALVA

Halva is a holiday candy that few children or adults in Syria can resist. The main ingredients in this version are sesame seeds and tahini (sesame seed paste). This recipe will make enough halva for everyone in most families to try. For more candy, just double the amount of each ingredient.

Ingredients

½ cup sesame seeds
¾ cup sugar
½ cup honey
1 tablespoon of water
½ cup tahini
1 tablespoon
  unsweetened lemon
  juice
cooking spray

Instructions

1. **Ask an adult** to help you with this recipe.
2. Preheat the oven to 400 degrees Fahrenheit. Spread the sesame seeds out evenly on an ungreased cookie sheet. Put the seeds into the oven and leave them for just a minute. Remove the seeds and stir them with a flat spatula. Taste a seed or two. If they're crunchy, they're done. If they're chewy, put them back in the oven for another minute or so. Keep doing this until the seeds are toasted, but not browned. Set the seeds aside to cool.
3. Mix together the honey, tahini, sugar, water, and lemon juice in a pan. Heat the mixture on the stove on medium heat until it bubbles. Keep simmering and stirring until the mixture thickens into a gooey paste. This could take ten or fifteen minutes, but don't overcook it. Be careful, the mixture will get very hot!
4. Remove the pan from the stove. Add the toasted sesame seeds to the pan and stir for several minutes. Make sure everything is mixed together well.
5. Spray a shallow glass dish or aluminum pie pan lightly with cooking spray. Pour the sticky mixture into the pan or dish. Spread it out evenly to a thickness of about a half an inch.
6. Let the halva sit for several hours. You can put it into a freezer if you don't want to wait so long. When it's solid and cool, cut the halva into bite-sized pieces and enjoy a sweet taste of Syria!

FRAME YOUR NAME IN ARABIC

To do this craft, you'll need a computer with access to the Internet. It's best if it's also attached to a printer. If you don't have a computer and printer at home, ask a teacher or librarian if you can use one at school or at the public library. However you do it, always ask permission from an adult before you begin any of the steps below.

Instructions

1. Go to Google Translate at http://translate.google.com. "Translate" means to change from one language into another.
2. Above the box on the left, where it lists the names of languages, click your own language, probably English. Above the box on the right click Arabic. If you don't see it listed, click the downward arrow, and click on Arabic in the list that appears.
3. Click inside the box on the left and type just your first name.
4. Do you see the odd looking squiggles in the box on the right? That's your name in Arabic letters. Unlike English, Arabic is written and read from right to left. So the first letter of your name is actually on the right. To hear what your name sounds like in Arabic, click on the speaker icon in the lower right corner of that box.
5. Using your mouse, highlight your Arabic name. Select "Copy" from your computer's "Edit" menu. If you don't know how to copy on your computer, go to "Help." Or ask an adult to show you how to do it.
6. Open Microsoft Word or some other word processing program. Many schools also have Print Shop or a similar program that allows you to change the size and look of letters.
7. Paste your Arabic name onto a blank page in Word (or some other program). Now you can use the program to change the size and color of your name. Again, ask for help if you don't know how to do this.
8. Once you learn what your computer can do, you can change the look of your name in many ways. Be creative! The "Word Art" function in Word offers lots of amazing choices. Use it if you can.
9. When you like what you see, print your name. Printers are all different. Some will only print in black and white. Others can print in color. Printing on colored paper is easy and gives a nice look even in black and white print. Craft stores sell all sorts of colorful papers. Many have borders and other fancy designs.
10. Frame your name. Prints of your friends' or family members' names also make fun gifts.

WHAT YOU SHOULD KNOW ABOUT SYRIA

Official name: Syrian Arab Republic

Population: about 18 million (July 2014 estimate does not include refugees currently living in other countries)

Capital city: Damascus (2.5 million people)

Largest city: Aleppo (about 3 million people)

Syria's major rivers: Barada, Euphrates, Orontes

Syria's highest point: Mt. Hermon (in the Anti-Lebanon Mountains), 9,232 feet (2,814 meters) above sea level

Syria's lowest point: Lake Tiberias (the Sea of Galilee near the Golan Heights) 656 feet (200 meters) below sea level

Religions: Sunni Muslim 74%, other Muslim 16%, Christian 10%

Official language: Arabic

Mountains: Anti-Lebanon, Jabal an-Nusayriyah, Jabal al-Druze

Syria's national anthem: "Humat ad-Diyar" ("Guardians of the Homeland")

UNESCO World Heritage Sites: the Crac des Chevaliers castle, Palmyra, the "Dead Cities," and the old sections of Damascus, Bosra, and Aleppo. All are listed as "at risk" now because of the present war in Syria.

Flag: The flag of the Syrian Arab Republic consists of three colors: red, white and black, with two green stars. It is divided into three rectangles of identical dimensions. Red is for the blood of those who fought for Syria's freedom. White represents the country's bright future. Black stands for the dark days of Syria's troubled past. The two stars once symbolized Syria and Egypt, when the two were joined as one country. Now it isn't clear what they stand for.

TIMELINE

BCE

ca. 9000	Early tribes settle along Syria's rivers.
ca. 3000	Ebla is built.
539	Syria becomes part of the Persian Empire.
332	Greek Emperor Alexander the Great conquers Syria.
64	Syria becomes part of the Roman Empire.

CE

395	Syria becomes part of the Byzantine Empire (eastern part of the Roman Empire).
613	Muhammad begins preaching new religion, Islam.
630s	Islamic warriors defeat Byzantine army, take control of Syria.
661–750	Umayyad caliphs rule Syria, make Damascus their capital.
750	Abbasid rulers move Islamic capital from Damascus to Baghdad.
1096–1300	The Crusades bring Christian warriors to Syria.
1192	Saladin and Richard the Lionheart sign a truce.
1516	Ottoman Empire takes control of Syria.
1918	Ottoman rule ends.
1920	Syria comes under the control of France.
1946	Syria becomes independent.
1958	Egypt and Syria join to form the United Arab Republic (UAR).
1961	UAR dissolved; Syria becomes independent nation again.
1963	Baath Party gains power over Syria.
1967	Six-Day War, Israel takes Golan Heights from Syria.
1971	Hafez al-Assad elected Syria's president.
1973	Syria adopts a new constitution.
1982	Attack by Syria's military on Muslim Brotherhood in Hama kills at least ten thousand people, including civilians.
1986	UK and US accuse Syria of supporting terrorists; countries break diplomatic relations.
1991	Syria fights in Gulf War against Iraq.
2000	President Hafez al-Assad dies; his son Bashar al-Assad is named president.
2011	Arab Spring protests begin in Syria and other Arab countries.
2012	United Nations calls for an end to violence; Syrian troops and rebels continue fighting.
2013	Groups fighting in Syria agree to meet in 2014 to talk about peace.
2014	Foreign fighters join Syrian groups in Syrian War; peace talks begin in Geneva, Switzerland.

CHAPTER NOTES

Introduction: Syria—Now and Then

1. Noah Rayman, *Time*, "Report: More Than 146,000 People Killed in Syrian Civil War," March 13, 2014. http://time.com/24077/syria-death-toll/

2. UNHCR, "Syria Regional Refugee Response." http://data.unhcr.org/syrianrefugees/regional.php

Chapter 1: A Day With Sabeen

1. Barbara Surk, *Christian Science Monitor*, "Syrian Refugee Children are Becoming the Family Breadwinners," November 29, 2013. http://www.csmonitor.com/World/Latest-News-Wires/2013/1129/Syrian-refugee-children-are-becoming-the-family-breadwinners

2. Ali Akbar Mahdi and Laila Hourani, "Syria," *Teen Life in the Middle East* (Westport, CT: Greenwood Press, 2003), pp. 191–192.

3. Ali Akbar Mahdi and Laila Hourani, "Syria," *Teen Life in the Middle East* (Westport, CT: Greenwood Press, 2003), p. 199.

4. Katherine Zoepf, *New York Times*, "Bestseller in the Mideast: Barbie With a Prayer Mat," September 22, 2005. http://www.nytimes.com/2005/09/22/international/middleeast/22doll.html

Chapter 2: Land of Sand and Water

1. Christina Phelps Grant, *The Syrian Desert* (New York: Macmillan Company, 1938), pp. 125–156, 159–174.

2. Abdul-Karim Rafeq, "Syrian Desert," in Philip Mattar, ed., *Encyclopedia of the Modern Middle East and North Africa* (New York: Macmillan Reference USA, 2004), p. 2136.

3. Robert Azzi, *National Geographic*, "Damascus: Syria's Uneasy Eden," vol. 45, no. 4, April 1974, p. 530.

4. Terry Carter, Lara Dunston, and Andrew Humphreys, *Syria & Lebanon* (Victoria, Australia: Lonely Planet, 2004), p. 15.

Chapter 3: The Past is the Present

1. Karen Armstrong, *Holy War: The Crusades and Their Impact on Today's World* (New York: Anchor Books, 2001), pp. 270–271.

2. Anthony Ham, et. al., *Middle East* (Victoria, Australia: Lonely Planet, 2012), p. 401.

3. Ibid., p. 419.

Chapter 4: A Government at War

1. Katherine Marsh and Ian Black, *The Guardian*, "Syria to Lift Emergency Rule After 48 Years—But Violence Continues," April 19, 2011. http://www.theguardian.com/world/2011/apr/19/syria-lift-emergency-rule-violence

2. David W. Lesch, *Syria: The Fall of the House of Assad* (New Haven, CT: Yale University Press, 2012), pp. 85–86.

3. Ibid., pp. 65–66.

4. Hugh Macleod, *Al Jazeera*, "Inside Deraa," April 19, 2011. http://www.aljazeera.com/indepth/features/2011/04/201141918352728300.html

5. BBC News, "Syria Uprising: UN Says Protest Death Toll Hits 3,000," October 14, 2011. http://www.bbc.co.uk/news/world-middle-east-15304741

6. Anne Barnard and Hwaida Saad, *New York Times*, "Shelling of Bus in Northern Syria Caps a Merciless Year," December 31, 2013. http://www.nytimes.com/2014/01/01/world/middleeast/syria.html?_r=0

7. UNHCR, "Syria Regional Refugee Response." http://data.unhcr.org/syrianrefugees/regional.php

8. Anne Barnard, *New York Times*, "After Shaky Beginning, Sides Report Progress at Syria Peace Talks," January 23, 2014. http://www.nytimes.com/2014/01/24/world/middleeast/Syria-Peace-Talks.html?ref=syria&_r=0

9. Zeina Karam, Associated Press, "500 Reported Killed in Rebel Infighting in Syria," January 10, 2014. http://bigstory.ap.org/article/syrian-army-kills-dozens-rebels-central-city

10. *New York Times*, "In Syria, Former Official Says, 'Nobody is Winning,'" January 18, 2014. http://www.nytimes.com/2014/01/19/world/middleeast/in-syria-former-official-says-nobody-is-winning.html?ref=syria&_r=0

Chapter 5: Religion

1. Ali Akbar Mahdi and Laila Hourani, "Syria," *Teen Life in the Middle East* (Westport, CT: Greenwood Press, 2003), p. 195.

2. Ibid., pp. 198-199.

3. US Department of State, "The International Religious Freedom Report 2006: Syria." http://www.state.gov/j/drl/rls/irf/2006/71432.htm

CHAPTER NOTES

4. Ali Akbar Mahdi and Laila Hourani, "Syria," *Teen Life in the Middle East* (Westport, CT: Greenwood Press, 2003), p. 204.

5. US Department of State, "The International Religious Freedom Report 2006: Syria." http://www.state.gov/j/drl/rls/irf/2006/71432.htm

6. Ben Hubbard, *World Post*, "Syria Crisis: Assad Makes Eid Al-Fitr Public Appearance," August 19, 2012. http://www.huffingtonpost.com/2012/08/19/assad-eid-al-fitr_n_1806394.html

7. Diana Darke, *Syria* (Guilford, CT: Globe Pequot Press, 2010), p. 117.

8. Brigid Keenan, *Damascus: Hidden Treasures of the Old City* (London: Thames & Hudson, 2001), p. 68.

9. David L. Kennedy and Andrew Peterson, *Saudi Aramco World*, "Guardians of the Pilgrim Wells: Damascus to Aqaba," January/February 2004, pp. 12–19. http://www.saudiaramcoworld.com/issue/200401/guardians.of.the.pilgrim.wells-damascus.to.aqaba.htm

10. Brigid Keenan, *Damascus: Hidden Treasures of the Old City* (London: Thames & Hudson, 2001), pp. 65–66.

11. Ibid,. p. 68.

12. Ibid., p. 69.

Chapter 6: People and Crafts

1. Central Intelligence Agency, *The World Factbook*, "Syria." https://www.cia.gov/library/publications/the-world-factbook/geos/sy.html

2. Thomas Collelo, ed., *Syria: A Country Study* (Washington: GPO for the Library of Congress, 1987).

3. Erika Solomon, Reuters, "Special Report—Amid Syria's Violence, Kurds Carve Out Autonomy," January 22, 2014. http://www.reuters.com/article/2014/01/22/syria-kurdistan-idUSL3N0KW3KY20140122

4. Golda Arthur, *BBC News Magazine*, "Aleppo Soap: War Threatens an Ancient Tradition," May 15, 2013. http://www.bbc.co.uk/news/magazine-22541698

5. Warwick Ball, *Syria: A Historical and Architectural Guide* (New York: Interlink Books, 1998), p. 200.

6. Kamel Al-Baba, "Calligraphy: A Noble Art," *Saudi Aramco World*, vol. 15, no. 4, July/August 1964, pp. 1–7.

7. Tim Stanley, *Palace and Mosque: Islamic Art from the Middle East* (London: V&A Publications, 2004), p. 78.

8. Shems, "Dabkeh—Palestine, Lebanon, Syria." http://www.shemsdance.com/articles/dabkeh-palestine-lebanon-syria/

9. Nancy Lindisfarne-Tapper and Bruce Ingham, eds., *Languages of Dress in the Middle East* (Surrey, England: Curzon Press, 1997), pp. 45, 64.

Chapter 7: Food and Holidays

1. Helen Corey, *The Art of Syrian Cookery* (Terre Haute, IN: CharLyn Publishing House, 1996), p. 20.

2. Ali Akbar Mahdi and Laila Hourani, "Syria," *Teen Life in the Middle East* (Westport, CT: Greenwood Press, 2003), p. 190.

3. May S. Bsisu, *The Arab Table: Recipes & Culinary Traditions* (New York: William Morrow, 2005), p. 259.

4. *Orange Blossom Water*, "Eid Al-Fitr, Sweets—2013," October 5, 2013. http://www.orangeblossomwater.net/index.php/2013/10/05/eid-al-fitr-sweets-2013/

5. Terry Carter, Lara Dunston, and Andrew Humphreys, *Syria & Lebanon* (Victoria, Australia: Lonely Planet, 2004), p. 66.

6. Ibid.

7. Clarissa Ward, CBS News, "Syria Refugees Fight for Survival in 'Dead Cities,'" April 4, 2013. http://www.cbsnews.com/news/syrian-refugees-fight-for-survival-in-dead-cities/

FURTHER READING

Books

Stanley, Diane. *Saladin: Noble Prince of Islam*. New York: HarperCollins, 2002.

Woog, Adam. *Creation of the Modern Middle East: Syria*. New York: Chelsea House Publishers, 2009.

Yomtov, Nel. *Syria: Enchantment of the World*. New York: Children's Press, 2014.

Zurlo, Tony. *Syria in the News: Past, Present, and Future*. Berkeley Heights, NJ: Enslow Publishers, 2006.

On the Internet

Fulla (dolls)
http://fulla.com/

Music of Syria
http://wn.com/music_of_syria

National Anthems: Syria
http://www.nationalanthems.me/syria-homat-el-diyar/

Sound Tourism: "Norias of Hama, Syria" (see and hear noria waterwheels)
http://www.sonicwonders.org/norias-of-hama-syria/

UNHCR: "Stories from Syrian Refugees"
http://data.unhcr.org/syrianrefugees/syria.php

Virtual Syria (take a virtual tour of Syria)
http://www.3dmekanlar.com/en/3d-syria.html

Works Consulted

Abadi, Jennifer Felicia. *A Fistful of Lentils: Syrian-Jewish Recipes from Grandma Fritzie's Kitchen*. Boston: Harvard Common Press, 2002.

Ajami, Fouad. *The Syrian Rebellion*. Stanford, CA: Hoover Institution Press, 2012.

Al-Baba, Kamel. "Calligraphy: A Noble Art." *Saudi Aramco World*, vol. 15, no. 4, July/August 1964, pp. 1-7.

Aleppo Food. "Sesame Halva." http://en.aleppofood.com/recipe/sesame-halva/#.UubsGBko7BI

Armstrong, Karen. *Holy War: The Crusades and Their Impact on Today's World*. New York: Anchor Books, 2001.

Armstrong, Karen. *Islam: A Short History*. New York: Modern Library, 2000.

Arthur, Golda. "Aleppo Soap: War Threatens an Ancient Tradition." *BBC News Magazine*, May 15, 2013. http://www.bbc.co.uk/news/magazine-22541698

Azzi, Robert. "Damascus: Syria's Uneasy Eden." *National Geographic*, vol. 45, no. 4, April 1974, pp. 512-531.

Ball, Warwick. *Syria: A Historical and Architectural Guide*. New York: Interlink Books, 1998.

Barnard, Anne. "After Shaky Beginning, Sides Report Progress at Syria Peace Talks." *New York Times*, January 23, 2014. http://www.nytimes.com/2014/01/24/world/middleeast/Syria-Peace-Talks.html?ref=syria&_r=0

Barnard, Anne, and Hwaida Saad. "Shelling of Bus in Northern Syria Caps a Merciless Year." *New York Times*, December 31, 2013. http://www.nytimes.com/2014/01/01/world/middleeast/syria.html?_r=0

BBC News. "Syria Uprising: UN Says Protest Death Toll Hits 3,000." October 14, 2011. http://www.bbc.co.uk/news/world-middle-east-15304741

Biography. "Bashar al-Assad." http://www.biography.com/people/bashar-al-assad-20878575

Bloom, Jonathan M., and Sheila S. Blair, eds. *The Grove Encyclopedia of Islamic Art and Architecture*. New York: Oxford University Press, 2009.

Brown, Ryan Lenora. "Syria's Children: Even Their First Words Are Now Shaped by War." *Christian Science Monitor*, March 13, 2013. http://www.csmonitor.com/World/Middle-East/2013/0313/Syria-s-children-even-their-first-words-are-now-shaped-by-war

Bsisu, May S. *The Arab Table: Recipes & Culinary Traditions*. New York: William Morrow, 2005.

Bulloch, John, and Harvey Morris. *No Friends But the Mountains: The Tragic History of the Kurds*. London: Oxford University Press, 1992.

Carter, Terry, Lara Dunston, and Andrew Humphreys. *Syria & Lebanon*. Victoria, Australia: Lonely Planet, 2004.

Central Intelligence Agency. *The World Factbook*. "Flags of the World." https://www.cia.gov/library/publications/the-world-factbook/docs/flagsoftheworld.html

Central Intelligence Agency. *The World Factbook*. "Syria." https://www.cia.gov/library/publications/the-world-factbook/geos/sy.html

Chaudhary, Suchitra Bajpai. "Hakawati: The Ancient Arab Art of Storytelling." *GulfNews*, November 19, 2010. http://gulfnews.com/life-style/culture/hakawati-the-ancient-arab-art-of-storytelling-1.712001

Collelo, Thomas, ed. *Syria: A Country Study*. Washington: GPO for the Library of Congress, 1987.

Corey, Helen. *The Art of Syrian Cookery*. Terre Haute, IN: CharLyn Publishing House, 1996.

Cross, Frank Moore. "The Origins of the Alphabet." *Ebla to Damascus: Art and Archaeology of Ancient Syria*. Washington, DC: Smithsonian Institution, 1985.

Darke, Diana. *Syria*. Guilford, CT: Globe Pequot Press, 2010.

Etheredge, Laura S., ed. *Middle East: Region in Transition, Syria, Lebanon and Jordan*. New York: Britannica Educational Publishing, 2011.

Fritzsche, Peter. *Hamsters: A Complete Pet Owner's Manual*. New York: Barron's, 2008.

Gerbino, Virginia Jerro, and Philip M. Kayal. *A Taste of Syria*. New York: Hippocrene Books, 2003.

Grant, Christina Phelps. *The Syrian Desert*. New York: Macmillan Company, 1938.

Gulevich, Tanya. *Understanding Islam and Muslim Traditions*. Detroit: Omnigraphics, 2004.

Ham, Anthony, et. al. *Middle East*. Victoria, Australia: Lonely Planet, 2012.

Hourani, Albert. *A History of the Arab Peoples*. Cambridge, MA: Belknap Press of Harvard University Press, 1991.

Hubbard, Ben. "Syria Crisis: Assad Makes Eid Al-Fitr Public Appearance." *World Post*, August 19, 2012. http://www.huffingtonpost.com/2012/08/19/assad-eid-al-fitr_n_1806394.html

Hussain, Saima S. *The Arab World Thought of It: Inventions, Innovations, and Amazing Facts*. New York: Annick Press, 2013.

Islamic Architecture. "Essential Architecture—Syria." http://www.islamic-architecture.info/WA-SY/WA-SY-001.htm

Karam, Zeina. "500 Reported Killed in Rebel Infighting in Syria." Associated Press, January 10, 2014. http://bigstory.ap.org/article/syrian-army-kills-dozens-rebels-central-city

FURTHER READING

Kaya, Ibrahim. "The Euphrates-Tigris Basin: An Overview and Opportunities for Cooperation under International Law." *Arid Lands Newsletter*, Fall/Winter 1998. http://ag.arizona.edu/OALS/ALN/aln44/kaya.html

Keenan, Brigid. *Damascus: Hidden Treasures of the Old City*. London: Thames & Hudson, 2001.

Kennedy, David L., and Andrew Peterson. "Guardians of the Pilgrim Wells: Damascus to Aqaba." *Saudi Aramco World*, January/February 2004, pp. 12-19. http://www.saudiaramcoworld.com/issue/200401/guardians.of.the.pilgrim.wells-damascus.to.aqaba.htm

LaFay, Howard. "Ebla: Splendor of an Unknown Empire." *National Geographic*, vol. 154, no. 6, December 1978, pp. 730-759.

LaFay, Howard. "Syria." *National Geographic*, vol. 154, no. 3, September 1978, pp. 326-361.

Lesch, David W. *Syria: The Fall of the House of Assad*. New Haven, CT: Yale University Press, 2012.

Levinson, David. *Encyclopedia of World Cultures*. Vol. 9. Boston: G.K. Hall and Company, 1995.

Lewis, Bernard. *The Middle East: A Brief History of the Last 2,000 Years*. New York: Scribner, 1995.

Lindisfarne-Tapper, Nancy, and Bruce Ingham. *Languages of Dress in the Middle East*. Surrey, England: Curzon Press, 1997.

Lunde, Paul. "Caravans to Mecca." *Saudi Aramco World*, vol. 25, no. 6, November/December 1974, pp. 2-3.

Maalouf, Amin. *The Crusades Though Arab Eyes*. Translated by Jon Rothschild. New York: Schocken Books, 1984.

Macleod, Hugh. "Inside Deraa." *Al Jazeera*, April 19, 2011. http://www.aljazeera.com/indepth/features/2011/04/201141918352728300.html

Mahdi, Ali Akbar, and Laila Hourani. "Syria." *Teen Life in the Middle East*. Westport, CT: Greenwood Press, 2003.

Marsh, Katherine, and Ian Black. "Syria to Lift Emergency Rule After 48 Years—But Violence Continues." *The Guardian*, April 19, 2011. http://www.theguardian.com/world/2011/apr/19/syria-lift-emergency-rule-violence

Mattar, Philip, ed. *Encyclopedia of the Modern Middle East and North Africa*. New York: Macmillan Reference USA, 2004.

Milgrom, Lionel. "Carbon Nanotubes: Saladin's Secret Weapon." Royal Society of Chemistry, November 15, 2006. http://www.rsc.org/chemistryworld/News/2006/November/15110602.asp

Lindisfarne-Tapper, Nancy, and Bruce Ingham, eds. *Languages of Dress in the Middle East*. Surrey, England: Curzon Press, 1997.

Mirali, N., R. Aziz, and I. Nabulsi. "Genetic Characterization of Rosa damascena Growing in Different Regions of Syria and Its Relationship to the Quality of the Essential Oils." *International Journal of Medicinal and Aromatic Plants*, March 2012, pp. 41-52.

Nelson, Nina. *Your Guide to Syria*. London: Alvin Redman, 1966.

New York Times. "In Syria, Former Official Says, 'Nobody is Winning.'" January 18, 2014. http://www.nytimes.com/2014/01/19/world/middleeast/in-syria-former-official-says-nobody-is-winning.html?ref=syria&_r=0

Orange Blossom Water. "Eid Al-Fitr, Sweets—2013." October 5, 2013. http://www.orangeblossomwater.net/index.php/2013/10/05/eid-al-fitr-sweets-2013/

Rayman, Noah. "Report: More Than 146,000 People Killed in Syrian Civil War." *Time*, March 13, 2014. http://time.com/24077/syria-death-toll/

Roden, Claudia. *The New Book of Middle Eastern Food*. New York: Alfred A. Knopf, 2000.

Rogan, Eugene. *The Arabs: A History*. New York: Basic Books, 2009.

Russell, George. "As UN Prepares for Mammoth Syria Aid Conference, Assad Regime Keeps Relief from the Suffering." FoxNews.com, January 7, 2014. http://www.foxnews.com/world/2014/01/07/as-un-prepares-for-mammoth-syria-aid-conference-assad-regime-keeps-relief-from/

Salloum, Habeeb. *The Arabian Nights Cookbook*. North Clarendon, VT: Tuttle Publishing, 2010.

Saudi Aramco World. "The Beehive Enigma." November/December 1967, pp. 8-9. http://www.saudiaramcoworld.com/issue/196706/the.beehive.enigma.htm

Schultz, Patricia. *1,000 Places to See Before You Die*. New York: Workman Publishing, 2011.

Shems. "Dabkeh—Palestine, Lebanon, Syria." http://www.shemsdance.com/articles/dabkeh-palestine-lebanon-syria/

Soguel, Dominique. "Schools Are Open For Syrian Refugees, But Most Can't Go Because They Can't Afford Pencils." *Huffington Post*, September 30, 2013. http://www.huffingtonpost.com/2013/09/30/syrian-refugees-schools-_n_4016833.html

Solomon, Erika. "Special Report—Amid Syria's Violence, Kurds Carve Out Autonomy." Reuters, January 22, 2014. http://www.reuters.com/article/2014/01/22/syria-kurdistan-idUSL3N0KW3KY20140122

Stanley, Tim. *Palace and Mosque: Islamic Art from the Middle East*. London: V&A Publications, 2004.

Surk, Barbara. "Syrian Refugee Children are Becoming the Family Breadwinners." *Christian Science Monitor*, November 29, 2013. http://www.csmonitor.com/World/Latest-News-Wires/2013/1129/Syrian-refugee-children-are-becoming-the-family-breadwinners

Syrian Arab News Agency. "Four Million Students Take 1st Term Exams in Defiance of Terrorism." January 5, 2014. http://sana.sy/eng/337/2014/01/05/520739.htm

UNHCR. "Syria Regional Refugee Response." http://data.unhcr.org/syrianrefugees/regional.php

US Department of State. "Profile." Syria, May 2007. http://www.state.gov/outofdate/bgn/syria/85051.htm

US Department of State. "The International Religious Freedom Report 2006: Syria." http://www.state.gov/j/drl/rls/irf/2006/71432.htm

US Energy Information Administration: Syria. "Overview/Data." February 18, 2014. http://www.eia.gov/countries/country-data.cfm?fips=SY

Ward, Clarissa. "Syria Refugees Fight for Survival in 'Dead Cities.'" CBS News, April 4, 2013. http://www.cbsnews.com/news/syrian-refugees-fight-for-survival-in-dead-cities/

Wright, Robin. *Dreams and Shadows: The Future of the Middle East*. New York: Penguin Press, 2008.

Zoepf, Katherine. "Bestseller in the Mideast: Barbie With a Prayer Mat." *New York Times*, September 22, 2005. http://www.nytimes.com/2005/09/22/international/middleeast/22doll.html

GLOSSARY

anti-Semitism (an-tahy-SEM-i-tiz-uhm)—Discrimination or prejudice towards Jews.

caliphate (KAL-uh-feyt)—The kingdom or empire ruled under an Islamic ruler or leader (caliph).

calligraphy (kuh-LIG-ruh-fee)—The art of fancy or decorative handwriting.

caravan (KAR-uh-van)—A group that travels together in the desert, often using camels to carry trade goods.

Hajj—The pilgrimage to Mecca; every Muslim must complete the Hajj at least once in his or her lifetime if able to do so.

hydroelectric (hahy-droh-i-LEK-trik)—Related to the creation of electricity from the energy produced by falling water.

irrigation (ir-i-GEY-shuhn)—Moving water from one place to another through pipes or ditches for the purpose of farming in dry areas.

mosque (mosk)—A Muslim place of worship and prayer.

nomad (NOH-mad)—A person without a permanent home who moves around together with a group based on food or pasture.

oasis (oh-WAY-sus)—A place where water flows into a desert, creating a fertile, green place of rest and refreshment for settlers or travelers.

ophthalmology (of-thuhl-MOL-uh-jee)—The medical science of the eye.

reforestation (ree-fawr-ist-AY-shun)—Replanting trees in places where forests have been cut down.

refugee (ref-yoo-JEE)—Someone who goes to another country or location seeking safety during a war or some other dangerous situation.

souk (sook)—A traditional Arab marketplace, made of many shops, stalls, and sellers.

INDEX

About the Author

Michael Capek is a former teacher and the author of many books for children and young adults. He loves to travel and write about the places he goes, as well as the places he wishes he could go. "Writing and reading are magic carpets to all sorts of wonderful places," he says. Michael lives on a farm in Kentucky, which he calls "my special corner of the world."

SYRIA